RUDYARD REFLE

A History and a Guide for Walkers

NORTH STAFFORDSHIRE RAILWAY.

Rudyard Lake

RUDYARD LAKE.

(STATION: RUDYARD. NORTH STAFFORDSHIRE RAILWAY).

Over 180 acres in extent. ♦ More than miles long. ♦ Situated amidst beautiful scenery.

BOATING AND FISHING.

BASIL JEUDA

CHURNET VALLEY BOOKS
6 Stanley Street, Leek, Staffordshire.ST13 5AG 01538 399033
email: picture.book@virgin.net web: freespace.virgin.net/c.hinton/

© Basil Jeuda and Churnet Valley Books 2001
ISBN 1 897949 74 X

1910 Advertising poster.   *Author's collection*

BOOK COVER: The Dam c1907   Unwin family collection

CHURNET VALLEY RAILWAY AND THE RUDYARD RESERVOIR.

Public Record Office

ACKNOWLEDGEMENTS

Many people have helped to make this book possible and I would like to thank the following:

British Waterways Board at Northwich and Gloucester, Horton Parish Council, Horton Church Council, Keele University Library, the Leek Post and Times, the Public Record Office at Kew, and the William Salt Library at Stafford for access to their records; the late George Bowyer, Alice Boulton, Derek Bowcock, Robert Cartwright, Christine Chester, Joan and the late Fred Cooper, John Davey, Len Hewitt, Vic Leese, Roy Lewis, the late George Lovenbury, Ray Perry, Jim Ridgway, David Salt and Frank Sutton; Camera Five Four and Tim Shuttleworth for their photographic support; Rudyard residents past and present for their memories and access to their memorabilia, and Christine Pemberton for processing the text, for the design and layout and for her advice and contributions. I have acknowledged separately the many people who have so generously allowed me to reproduce their photographs and plans.

Finally, I would like to thank my wife, Laura, for the continued support she gives to my writing.

Basil Jeuda. Macclesfield
March 2001

CONTENTS

Two views of the drained Rudyard Lake in 1982. View from the Leek to Macclesfield road looking towards the north end of the Lake. This gives an impression of how the Vale of Rudyerd looked in the late 1790s, before it was flooded to create the reservoir.   *Christine Pemberton*

1982 view from Horton Lodge boathouse across the Lake; in the foreground is the meandering Dunsmore Brook and in the background can be seen Moreton's fishing hut, used by the Sea Scouts.

Christine Pemberton

INTRODUCTION

My interest in Rudyard Lake originated from my lengthy research, spanning more than twenty years, into the history of the North Staffordshire Railway and the railway lines it owned and worked, together with the network of canals this railway operated following its purchase in 1847 of the Trent & Mersey Canal for £1,170,000.

From the standpoint of social and economic history, I began researching the impact that this canal system and its feeder reservoirs had on the development of two villages - the first was Rudyard/Horton, from which was published *Rudyard Lake - The Bicentenary 1797-1997* in March 1997, and the second was Caldon Low, from which came *The Limestone Quarries of Caldon Low*, published in October 2000.

I think that it is fair to say that the Rudyard Lake book was intended to be a definitive history of the Lake, and those potential readers who have yet to read it I would encourage to do so.

This book, which moves the history forward by four years, contains a shorter version of the history of the Lake, but contains new material drawn from further research I have carried out in recent years. I also thought it helpful for those walking round the Lake to have a pictorial interpretation of how the Lake, Lake Road, the Dam and the railway stations looked in days gone by, and to be able to compare the past with the present. Rudyard was much photographed down the years and I have included many photographs not previously published; I have used a small number of photographs that appeared in the first book purely for the sake of historical completeness.

A 1908 John Valentine postcard looking south showing the centre of the Lake.

Author's collection

1905 view from the Macclesfield to Leek road looking south, with Horton Lodge boathouse in the centre and the Dam just visible in the background.

Author's collection

An early 1920s view taken from above Reacliffe Road, looking south down onto the Dam.

Author's collection

Real Photo. Copyright H. Breaks, Rudyard. Rudyard Lake and the Cloud, 1,100. FT

An early 1920s view looking down from the Leek to Macclesfield road. Two boathouses, Challinor's and the Lady of the Lake, built in the 1890s can be seen.

Author's collection

Another 1920s view looking from above the Leek to Macclesfield road towards Bosley Cloud. On the west side of the Lake can be seen several of the holes of Rudyard Lake Golf Club.

Author's collection

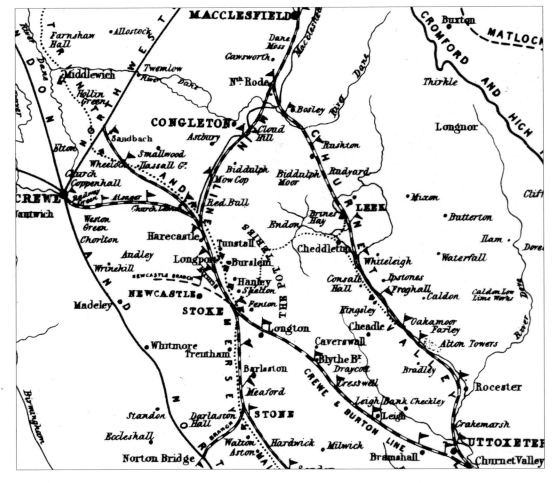

1849 map of the North Staffordshire Railway showing the Churnet Valley Railway which opened in that year. Stations are clearly marked with a flag; Rudyard's station opened on 22 July 1850. The dotted line illustrates the course of the Trent & Mersey Canal system from Leek and Froghall to Shelton (Etruria).
The late Robert Keys collection

Extract from an 1823 receipt book showing land taken for the reservoir.
Christine Chester collection

HISTORY

Built between 1797 and 1800, the Reservoir at Rudyard owes its origins to the fact that at the end of the 18th Century the Trent & Mersey Canal Company was regularly running out of water to serve the Caldon and Trent & Mersey canals. These canals were becoming more intensively used. Caldon Quarries were producing more limestone, nearly all of which was transported along the canal, and output had increased from nothing in 1777 to 48,220 tons by 1794 and to 116,276 tons in 1848, after which the Churnet Valley Railway was opened and the limestone was also carried by rail. The route of the Caldon Canal, 17½ miles from Froghall to Etruria, became increasingly industrialised, with, for example, limekilns at Froghall from 1778, flint mills at Consall from 1778 (the former forge) and from 1811 (Crowgutter), and three different sets of limekilns in the Cheddleton area by 1816, all testifying to the increasing demand for water to run the canal system.

Within a few years of the opening of the Caldon Canal, the Trent & Mersey Canal Company had sought to improve the supply of water through the building of reservoirs at Knypersley in 1782/83, and at Stanley Pool and Bagnall Reservoir in 1786/89. Despite this the North Staffordshire canal system and its reservoirs suffered shortages in every year between 1788 and 1796. This in turn led to the first attempt to introduce a Bill in Parliament in 1795/96 to construct a canal from Endon to Leek, a 2½ mile feeder channel from the Vale of Rudyerd (as it was then called) to Leek itself, and a Reservoir at Rudyard. The 1795/96 Bill did not pass through Parliament, but the 1796/97 one was successful and secured Parliamentary approval in March 1797.

Whilst the concept of a reservoir was sound enough, the reliance on local streams to fill it was flawed; this, in turn, led to the construction of another feeder channel, this time from Dane Bridge to the north end of the reservoir via Rushton, under an 1809 Act of Parliament. Whilst this met immediate needs, the opening of the second Harecastle Tunnel, in order to cope with the increasing traffic, placed further demands upon the reservoir system. An 1823 Act granted powers to the Canal Company to deepen the Dane feeder and to lower the weir at the Dane Bridge paper mill. Until the arrival of the North Staffordshire Railway's construction of the Churnet Valley Railway alongside the Lake in 1847, and the deepening of the Lake by the NSR after the 1904 Act, the basic engineering to and for the Lake had been completed by 1823.

There are occasions when it is possible to gain some insight into how the Vale of Rudyerd looked before it was flooded in 1801 and the Leek Canal was opened in the spring of that same year. In summers of severe drought, when the reservoir has run dry, if one stands in the layby on the A523, south of Rushton on the Macclesfield to Leek road, and looks across to Cliffe Park Hall you will get a good impression of how the Vale of Rudyerd appeared prior to the construction of the reservoir in 1797. Barnslee Farm, built by 1727, is typical of the older properties in this area, whilst Cliffe Park Hall, built in 1811 by John Haworth, was the first major new property to overlook the recently constructed reservoir.

The area now commonly referred to as Rudyard is centred around Harper's Gate and goes down to the Lake. The old Township boundaries place Rudyard itself east of Dunsmore Brook, a brook which meanders in the bed of the reservoir. This brook served as a boundary to the estate of the Earl of Macclesfield, whose farms and cottages were sold by auction in 1919. Rudyard, along with the settlements of Horton and Gratton, form part of the parish of Horton. The major physical changes, new housing development and, between 1900 and 1930, café development, have largely taken place around Harper's Gate where the former Poacher's Tavern (Station Hotel) is located. The Jubilee Stone, quarried from Nixon's quarry on Horton Bank, dates from Queen Victoria's Jubilee in 1897.

Walking around the Harper's Gate area and along Dunwood Lane and the Lake Road, it is reasonably straightforward to relate the various stages of physical development that have taken place in the last 150 years, and also the reasons for them. Older cottage property dating back to the 18th century can be seen along Dunwood Lane, including Sunnybank and Dumpling Cottage, and evidence of part of Greenlands, converted by William Sandeman in 1897, can be seen in the central section of this property.

Later development along Dunwood Lane - Rock Cottage, Hawthorn Cottage and Woodlands in particular - reflect the development of the Harper's Gate area as potentially attractive commuter village for Leek and the Potteries as middle class professional people began to arrive.

A date stone of 1610 can be seen on the Dunwood Lane side of the Poacher's Tavern and, certainly by the early part of the 19th century, if not much earlier, this building had become a tavern, with its convenient location at the junction of the roads to Biddulph, Leek and Endon; an 1851 Guide to Rudyard Lake and Alton Towers refers to "two small public houses, almost opposite each other", the other being Rock House. With the arrival of Stephen Chesters-Thompson at Horton Lodge, which he built in 1890, this prominent Manchester brewer-politician arranged for his family concern, Chesters Brewery, to purchase what was then called the Railway Hotel, and major extensions were carried out between 1892 and 1897.

The variety of houses that can be seen along Lake Road reflect various attempts by local landowners to sell parcels for 'villa' development. Larger plots were made available in an 1873 Auction, but without success and this was followed by an 1880 Auction of smaller plots along Lake Road; Vine Cottage and Rose Cottage have date stones of 1884 and 1881 respectively. Fern Cottage and Underwood were both built by 1884. The 1890 Auction, offering large plots of land running from Lake Road towards the Lake produced only one large development, The Knoll, erected in 1894/95 for local estate agent and valuer John Brealey, but smaller plots were sold and Pine Cottage (1892), Sylvian House (1893), and Albury House (1896) evidence this. The smaller cottages were occupied by people in trade and domestic service, who would supplement their income by selling teas and later, storing bicycles.

With the aggressive promotion, by the NSR, of Rudyard as a place to stay, the 1890s saw several houses built to provide accommodation as well as teas. A fine example of this is Pine Cottage, built by Frank Salt in 1892. Prior to the construction of the more convenient St Gabriel's Church on Horton Bank in 1904/05, services were held for some years at Albury House, which, like Pine Cottage, was built by Frank Salt.

At the cross roads a significant commercial investment was made by Hugo Sleigh, of the well known Leek family, when he built Holly Bank (now known as Camrose Hall) in 1891; 'accommodation' was offered and in addition, at ground level, three lock up shops, which survived into the 1960s. Elsewhere along Lake Road the four houses known as The Beeches, also built on plots of land sold in 1890, offered tourist accommodation.

It was just after the First World War, as an extension to the furthest house of The Beeches, that Rudyard's largest café, Woodside, was built by the Coxon family; it finally closed in 1973 and newer houses were built on the site in 1986/87.

At the side of Wynforde, which along with Glenwood and the Wesleyan Chapel were built on plots sold in 1910, can still be seen the wooden Limes café, built by the Guilliard family in 1906. This was the first purpose built café on Lake Road.

The Hotel Rudyard started as a water bailiff's cottage when the reservoir was constructed, and if one looks carefully from the hotel car park, one can still discern part of the original cottage; there were several extensions and alterations over the years, the most important being in 1906/07, with the addition of another storey, and the difference in the way in which the stone has weathered is clearly visible from the front of the hotel; the outbuildings, which date back to at least 1873 have, in days gone by, seen use as a mortuary, where people who had drowned in the Lake were laid out. Red Cottage and Lilac Cottage are other examples of surviving 18th century cottages. Beyond the hotel car park on the right can be seen the replacement water bailiff's house, built in 1852, facing which is the 18th century stone Yew Tree Cottage. The road from the Poacher's Tavern was described in 1851 as "rough craggy" - a condition which can be seen in postcards of the Edwardian era. It was here that Brassington's built a café c1930 and continued in business until the mid 1980s. Facing the hotel car park was Kingswood, a small village store opened by Tommy Stone in 1923; it was demolished in the 1980s to be replaced by new houses.

Away from the Lake some significant properties with views to the Lake were built; Rudyard Villa in 1861 for Matthew Gaunt, but its view was 'spited' by the erection of Spite Hall in the early 1860s, built as a gamekeeper's cottage. Fair View was built for Hanley wine merchant John Munro in 1879 and Horton Lodge for Stephen Chesters-Thompson in 1890. Those promoting villa developments in the late 19th century were never able to encourage others to build similar properties.

Historically the economy of Horton, Harper's Gate and Rudyard was one of agriculture, with many large, and mainly tenanted, farms predominating. This provided direct employment for much of the local community, with additional employment coming for blacksmiths, dressmakers and people "in service". There was also a small scale quarrying operation on Whorrocks Bank (Horton Road), one adjacent to Foxholes and another (fallen into disuse by c1849) on the site of what was to become Rudyard station. The construction of the Reservoir led to the employment of two water bailiffs - one at the Dam and the other on the Dane Feeder, near Wincle; later the Canal Company also employed labourers. The location attracted a growing middle class, commuting from Leek and the Potteries by rail, and this increasing population supported new churches, St Gabriel's on Horton Road (1905) and the Wesleyan Chapel on Lake Road (1912). Village facilities included a Post Office, at various locations around Harper's Gate, the Memorial Institute, where pantomimes were held for many years, which opened in 1922, together with the Tennis Club in the same year, located in the field on the eastern side of the railway line.

Why did, and still do, so many people come to Rudyard Lake? Looking back to the start of the tourist era, heralded by the arrival of the railway in 1849, and the opening of the station at the south end of the Lake on 22 July 1850, the attraction was the sheer beauty and tranquillity of the surrounding countryside. From the outset the NSR sought to provide comfort and facilities for the visitors; well laid walks were constructed in 1850 and seating installed so that *"Pic-nic parties may here partake of refreshments in a very agreeable manner ...It is not an unusual occurrence for the casual visitor to the Lake to meet with groups of from twenty to fifty people (chiefly females from Leek) seated around tables on the green sward before the door of some humble cottage, drinking tea."* By then living in Bombay, the parents of Rudyard Kipling, who had spent many happy hours at Rudyard, named their son after the Lake. With the passing of the 1904 Act, the NSR constructed several footpaths, principally on the west bank at the north end of the Lake, and these were popularly featured in the NSR 'official' postcards of the time.

The NSR, initially in 1851, sought to provide entertainment on the Lake itself, but this endeavour was thwarted by Fanny Bostock, owner of Cliffe Park Hall, following her instigation of a High Court Action against the NSR. These proceedings dragged on from 1851 to 1856 and resulted in the NSR being restricted from holding events upon the Lake. This injunction remained in force until it was overthrown by the 1904 Act of Parliament. After 1904 regattas and galas became a regular feature in the years up to and shortly beyond, the First World War.

The NSR sought to circumvent the restriction by organising events at the Lakeside - such as the arrival of the African Blondin in 1864, annual well dressing ceremonies from 1871, which continued for some twenty years, and the appearance of Captain Webb in 1877; they also encouraged special events at the Hotel Rudyard, developed in 1851 from the original water bailiff's cottage and successively enlarged and improved down to 1907. A new ball room was opened in 1873 and in 1876 roller skating was introduced in the grounds of the Hotel Rudyard and continued for some years.

With the passing on the 1904 Act, which granted powers to raise the level of the Lake, to run boats and to develop a Hotel and provide other facilities, the NSR forged a commercial and entrepreneurial spirit, adding a floor on to the Hotel, opening chalets at the north end of the Lake and providing boats for hire, together with a landing stage at the Dam, which it leased to John Hall. In 1905 the Lake was restocked with fish, and a roller skating rink was built and leased to Elite Skating in 1909. In 1905 it opened a second station at the north end of the Lake and purchased Rudyard Villa c1908.

The NSR actively promoted the Rudyard Lake Golf Club - with its presence strongly felt on the Board of Management - and leased Cliffe Park Hall and its Estate, acquired by the NSR in 1904, as a residential club house and course. From its opening in 1906 as a nine-hole golf course, located mainly in front of Cliffe Park Hall, it expanded into an 18-hole course in 1908, using land behind Barnslee, where the original tees and greens can still be seen. Until the outbreak of the First World War in 1914, the Club was amongst the most successful in North Staffordshire, but with declining membership from 1918 onwards, the Club fell on hard times and the NSR distanced itself completely, eventually calling in a financial guarantee from Mr Jones, Financial Director of Wardle and Davenport for £500 in respect of unpaid rent for the Club House. The Golf Club finally folded in 1926.

The number of refreshment facilities increased steadily; occupants of many of the older 18th and 19th century properties would provide tea and refreshments. As new houses were built on Lake Road - Pine Cottage being the first in 1892 - the villagers also began to offer accommodation and storage facilities for bicycles. With Rudyard's growing popularity further tearooms - Abberley's on Dunwood Lane c1900, the Guilliards' Limes Café in 1906 and the Coxon's Woodside Café from 1912 - all moved into the area from elsewhere.

Away from the Lakeside, at Spite Hall, tea rooms and accommodation were developed from modest beginnings in 1873, with the expansion and conversion of a gamekeeper's cottage over a 30 year period. The fields in front of Spite Hall provided ample accommodation for Sunday School outings, wedding receptions and trade union demonstrations. Along Reacliffe Road and at the north end of the Lake wooden chalets started to appear from 1910 onwards; very few still survive in their original form, but many have been converted, with some of the original timbers just visible.

Rudyard continued to be a popular tourist destination for visitors from the traditional areas of Leek, Macclesfield and the Potteries in the 1920s and 1930s, but there were fewer railway excursions from further afield. The pleasure gardens at Alton Towers had now become increasingly popular after their re-opening in April 1924. From around 1910 Rudyard began to attract a growing number of visitors who arrived by road; charabanc, bus, motor bikes and cycles increasingly clogged the narrow roads and lanes. Following an accident c1913 the 18th century cottages facing the Station Hotel (Poacher's Tavern) were demolished to make way for a road-widening scheme.

Who else used the Lake? The boating rights were restricted by law to those with riparian rights (that is, those who owned or leased the banks of the Lake). With a small number of such landowners, there were few boathouses until the 1890s, when Horton Lodge, Lady of the Lake and Challinor's were built; 'infilling' between these main boathouses has continued ever since. Four were built c1900 south of the Horton Lodge boathouse adjacent to the Heath's double boathouse. The Brackens and Bilton boathouses just north of the Lady of the Lake were built c1900 and a succession of little boathouses have been constructed ever since, with distinctive and clashing architecture.

The Second World War saw wires strung across the lake to prevent enemy landings, whilst the wooded slopes provided excellent training facilities for jungle warfare. American troops, stationed at nearby Blackshaw Moor, prepared for the 1944 D-Day landings in Normandy by exercising amphibious landing crafts at the north end of the lake.

Since its modest beginnings in 1956 the Rudyard Lake Sailing Club has had significant usage of the Lake. There has been little organised swimming on the Lake, as it is considered dangerous. Angling has always been popular with angling clubs - The Macclesfield United Anglers' Society and its successor clubs, Ye Olde Angling Cub at the north end has fished there since at least the 1870s, whilst the Rudyard Angling Club was started in 1953. The 89th Stoke on Trent Sea Scouts were established in 1936 on the east bank of the Lake. The Potteries Paddlers Canoeing Club established a base at the Lake in 1986/87. Club rowing has been a feature of the Lake in recent years. The miniature railway was opened by Peter Hanton in 1985, running for 1½ miles along the east bank of the Lake.

My earlier Rudyard book took the history to the beginning of 1997. During that year numerous events celebrated the Bicentenary of the Lake. The Celebration Dinner at the Hotel Rudyard was held on 27 March, the Historical Weekend and Exhibition on 17/18

May, the Rudyard Regatta on 14/15 June and a Flower Arranging Competition at the Leek and District Show on 26 July. Visitors from Rudyard, Montana, USA were welcomed.

Since 1997 the major initiative at the Dam has been the conversion of the Trent & Mersey Canal Boathouse on the west shore of the Lake which, with the erection of new toilet and changing room facilities, is estimated to cost around £200,000. This project has been driven forward by Ray Perry and his fellow Trustees of the Rudyard Lake Trust, which was established on 20 June 1996. The Trust looked at the earlier plans of the 1980s for converting the Boathouse and for which outline planning permission had been granted. New plans for toilets and the conversion of the Boathouse into a Visitor Centre were approved by Staffordshire Moorlands District Council in April and July 1998. A funding package of around £200,000 was put together with grants from the European Commission, British Waterways, Rudyard Lake Trust and the Rudyard League of Friends, the Heritage Lottery Fund, the Staffordshire Environmental Fund and Advantage West Midlands. The project has been carried out in three phases - first the new toilet block and changing rooms, at a cost of £70,000, secondly the underpinning works to the boathouse at a cost of c£15,000 and thirdly the conversion of the boathouse to a Visitor Centre at a cost of £115,000. The toilet block was officially opened on 5 November 2000 by Barbara Adams, the well known BBC Radio Stoke presenter. At the time of writing the new Visitor Centre is scheduled for opening on Easter Sunday, April 2001.

The Boat Store was replaced in October 1997 by temporary facilities which included a café, ranger store and boat racks. This is intended to be a temporary arrangement, with short term planning consent for five years. Outline drawings have been prepared for a snack bar, kitchen, ranger office, office for the Friends, 16 boat racks, two boat bays and facilities for disabled people. Both the current rowing clubs - the Staffordshire University Rowing Club and the North Staffordshire Rowing Club - are experiencing a considerable increase in interest in the sport, with the consequent need to accommodate more boats. The possibility of outrigger canoeing for people with various types of disability has been actively explored and the University Rowing Club and Horton Lodge Special School have recently been given an 'Awards For All' grant of £5,000 for the purchase of a canoe.

In order to encourage a return to leisure rowing, Rudyard Lake Limited, the private company managing the Lake, purchased ten rowing boats from Regents Park, London; these have all been well patronised, but regulations have been introduced to prevent rowing at the northern end in the interests of wildlife conservation.

Exciting developments have been taking place in the past four years at the Rudyard Lake Sailing Club. The £750,000 scheme consists of a new Club House, which will be fully accessible for disabled sailors. There is a meeting room for the local community and independent access down to the Lake for people with disabilities; a training centre for youth and disabled groups; the rutted Reacliffe Road has been purchased from British Rail. This carriage drive was acquired by the NSR in 1904, along with the Cliffe Park Estate. A new ¾ mile water main to connect with the sailing club is being installed.

Funding is largely coming from the Lottery Fund and from Leader II funds from the European Commission. Sponsorship has also come from the Foundation for Sports and Arts, the Staffordshire Moorlands District Council, the Lords Taverners, Sportsmatch; and the efforts of volunteers from the Club have been worth £60,000. The scene is now set for the Club to become one of the leading sailing clubs in the Midlands.

Whilst the number of angling clubs visiting the Lake has declined slightly - the numbers actually engaged in match angling at the Lake has, in recent years, dropped by almost 50% - it seems to be due to the changing fashion in angling and it is hoped that the trend will be reversed.

For the benefit of the public four interpretation panels, sponsored in part by the Tourist Board, have been erected around the Lake to provide visitors with a better understanding of the Lake's history and wildlife.

The activities of the Sea Scouts and the Potteries Paddlers remain popular, whilst the Lake regularly hosts outdoor pursuits both for private organisations and the Army.

In recent years an Action Group centred around the Parish of Horton - encompassing the settlements of Horton, Gratton and Rudyard - has been established and this led to the Original Horton Action Plan being adopted by the Parish at a public meeting on 10 June 1998. In consequence the Parish has been able to access government funding to enhance the quality of life for this rural community. This process was known as 'Leader' funding and has now been replaced by a fund of £3.75 million for Rural North East Staffordshire. The individual projects for which funding has been obtained include the Rudyard Lake Visitor Centre, Rudyard Lake Festivals 1999 and 2000, Interpretation Panels, the RGH United Mosaic project, an adventure garden at Horton Lodge school, a community room at the Sailing Club and improvements to Horton Village Hall. A Millennium Committee for the Parish oversaw the erection of a standing stone and time capsule at the Dam Head.

The Rudyard Lake League of Friends was established on 25 September 1998, with Viviane Lowe as Chairman. Its remit was threefold. First, to organise educational programmes to increase the appreciation of the Lake, its history and development and its wildlife and habitat. Secondly, to arrange and encourage events, working with others, to stimulate greater use and enjoyment of the Lake. Thirdly, to organise fundraising to help finance improvements to the Lake. The friends, now with over 100 members, has gone from strength to strength and its volunteer initiatives are already making an impact on the Lake, its amenities and environment.

The Poacher's Tavern has been closed to the public for some time, as attempts are made to secure planning approval and obtain funding for residential development. If this proves successful it will see the end to the tradition of an ale house at Harper's Gate which stretches back two hundred years or more. The village lost its post office at Rock House at the end of March 1997.

In 1999 a small group, linked to the Macclesfield Canal Society, felt that consideration should be given to promoting an earlier canal scheme, dating back to 1811, to link the Macclesfield Canal from Bosley with the Caldon Canal at Endon - the route going via Rudyard but not over the Lake. The scheme has its supporters as well as its detractors and has not yet reached the stage of public consultation.

In November 2000 the popular Rudyard Lake Railway changed hands, with Peter Hanton, who had developed the railway since 1985, selling to Mike Hanson and his partner Eileen Turpin. Their current proposals are to operate the line every Sunday, the last Saturday each month and bank holiday weekends.

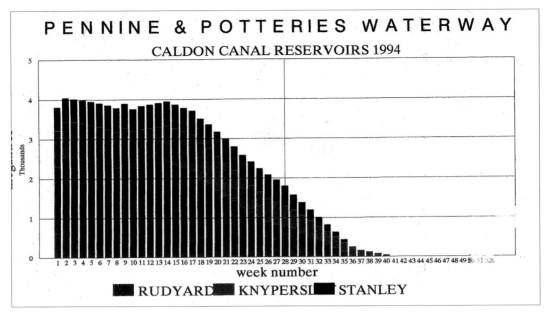

Rudyard Lake was built as a reservoir to feed the canal system in North Staffordshire - successively the Leek Canal, the Caldon Canal and the Trent & Mersey Canal. Now more than 200 years on it is still fulfilling its original purpose. being one of several local reservoirs to do so. This 1994 chart shows the drawing down of water from Rudyard, Knypersley and Stanley in the April to October period, and the relative importance of the Rudyard reservoir in providing water for the local canal system.

British Waterways

The fish ladders on the River Dane, near Wincle c1900.

Author's collection

Gig Hall in the Dane Valley c1900. This is the point where the flow of water from the River Dane is split, with water flowing along the feeder to Rushton and Rudyard Lake, as well as flowing to Congleton, thence Northwich.

Author's collection

Dane River, Nr. Macclesfield.

A delightful view, looking east, of the Feeder Cottage in the Dane Valley c1905. Built in the early 19th century for the water bailiff, it was last occupied by a water bailiff in 1959, and was sold by British Waterways in 1995.

Author's collection

Royal Oak, Rushton, on the Leek to Macclesfield Road c1920. The feeder flows under the road to the left and in front of the pub.
Author's collection

The feeder just south of the Dam c1900, with the footpath leading up to the Hotel Rudyard just visible in the background.
Author's collection

A view from the feeder c1915 looking north towards Dunwood Lane. Left is Woodfield Cottage, in the centre left is Sunnybank and its café. Far right is the Station Hotel.

Author's collection

John Haworth, who built Cliffe Park Hall in 1811 at an estimated cost of £25,000.
Chrsitine Chester collection

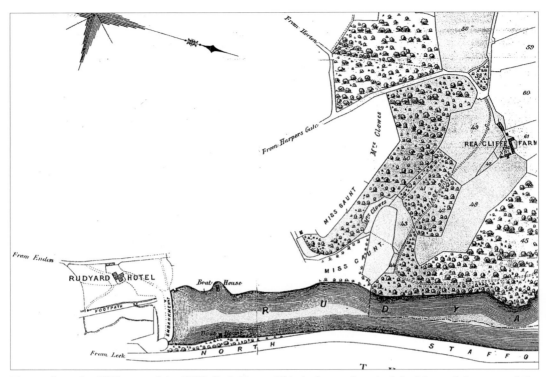

Extract from the 1875 map of the Cliffe Park Estate. This is the south end of the lake and the route of the Feeder to Leek can be seen. Note the location of the Boathouse in the small bay - this was replaced a few years later by what is now the Visitor Centre.   *Christine Chester collection*

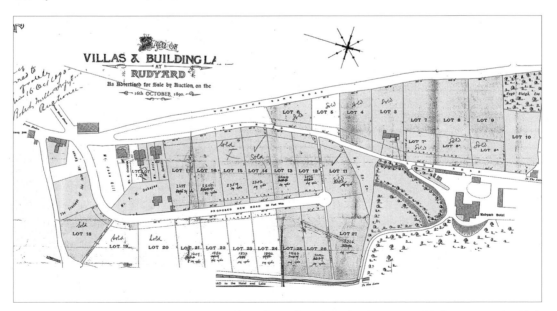

1890 Auction Catalogue showing the plots being offered for sale. Note the new road being proposed, which was only partially constructed. The catalogue shows properties around Harper's Gate and the buildings of Hotel Rudyard.   *Author's collection*

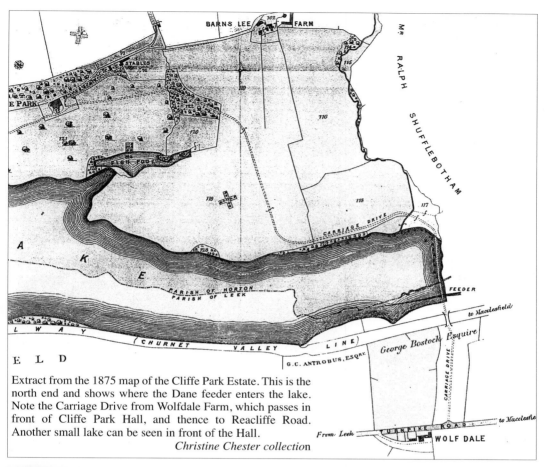

Extract from the 1875 map of the Cliffe Park Estate. This is the north end and shows where the Dane feeder enters the lake. Note the Carriage Drive from Wolfdale Farm, which passes in front of Cliffe Park Hall, and thence to Reacliffe Road. Another small lake can be seen in front of the Hall.

Christine Chester collection

Surviving 18th century cottages on Dunwood Lane.

Author's collection

The Abberley family at Sunnybank, on Dunwood Lane in 1922. This cottage was built in 1757 and John James Abberley moved to Harper's Gate c1900 as a cobbler and later as a baker.   *Abberley family collection*

William Sandeman, photographer and postcard publisher, moved to Greenlands, on Dunwood Lane, in 1896. The original 18th century cottage can be seen in the centre.   *The late Alan Wincle collection*

11

EXCURSIONS FROM NOTTINGHAM & TRENT
TO
TUTBURY, ALTON, RUDYARD, AND ASHBOURNE FOR DOVEDALE,
EVERY SATURDAY, UNTIL OCTOBER 6th.

CHEAP RETURN TICKETS will be issued on Saturdays, from Nottingham and Trent, to Tutbury, Rudyard, and Ashbourne for Dovedale, available to return on the following Monday or Tuesday, at the undermentioned low fares for the double journey, viz:—

	CLASS	1st	3rd
Tutbury		5/0	2/6
Ashbourne		7/0	3/6
Alton		7/0	3/6
Rudyard		8/0	4/0

The Tickets are available to Rudyard by the through Train leaving Nottingham at 6 10 p.m.; to Ashbourne at 1 35, and 6 10 p.m.; and to Tutbury at 8 20 a.m., 1 35, and 6 10 p.m.; returning from Rudyard at 10 55 a.m., 1 21, and 5 54 p.m.; Alton at 11 27 a.m., 1 55, and 6 51 p.m.; Ashbourne at 11 0 a.m., 1 40, and 6 15 p.m., and Tutbury at 12 17, 2 47, and 7 12 p.m.

CHILDREN UNDER 12 YEARS OF AGE HALF-PRICE.

CHEAP HALF-HOLIDAY EXCURSIONS TO RUDYARD,
EVERY MONDAY, THURSDAY, & SATURDAY, UNTIL FURTHER NOTICE.

STATIONS AND TIMES OF DEPARTURE		Rudyard			STATIONS AND TIMES OF DEPARTURE		Rudyard		
	CLASS	1st	2nd	3rd		CLASS	1st	2nd	3rd
Harecastle	1 43 p.m				Etruria	2 20 p.m.			
Longport	1 51 „				Newcastle	2 15 „			
Tunstall	2 4 „	3/0	2/0	1/6	Longton	2 20 „	3/0	2/0	1/6
Burslem	2 8 „				Fenton	2 23 „ p.m.			
Cobridge	2 11 „				Stoke	2 35 & 5 20			
Hanley	2 15 „				Bucknall	2 43 & 5 28	3/0	2/0	1/3

RETURNING FROM RUDYARD AT 8 50 P.M.

ALSO, EVERY MONDAY, WEDNESDAY AND SATURDAY.

		Fares for the Double Journey.
		1st Class 2nd Class 3rd Class

Leave Macclesfield (Hibel Road) at 10 27 a.m., 12 50 and 3 43 p.m.
" " (Central) at 10 29 a.m., 12 52 and 3 45 p.m. ... ... } 3/0   2/0   1/3
RETURNING FROM RUDYARD AT 6 21 AND 8 23 P.M.

Children under 12 years of age half-price.

These Tickets are issued upon the express condition, that they are available for the Stations only named thereon, and if used for any other Stations they will be forfeited, and the full Ordinary Fare charged.

ALTON GARDENS.

The GARDENS of Alton Towers are now RE-OPENED for the Season, and Pleasure Parties will be admitted on any Week-day, on the usual terms.
Tickets for Alton can be obtained on application at the Stations.

Extract from 1877 North Staffordshire Railway timetable, advertising excursions and fares to Rudyard.

Author's collection

Station Hotel as viewed from Dunwood Lane c1914. The early 17th century building can be seen in the centre with later additions in the form of the two upper floors. The Chesters Brewery extensions of the mid 1890s are to the left.

Roy Lewis collection

Station Hotel c1910 with the original 1610 buildings and old ale house on the right and at the back. To the front is the mid-1890s Chesters Brewery extension.

Author's collection

Harper's Gate 1902, with the 18th century cottages on the right, one of which housed the Post office. These cottages were demolished c1913 as part of a road widening scheme. Facing is Rock House (an ale house in the 1850s) and Ivy Cottage. The Jubilee Stone, erected in 1897, is at the junction of Horton Road and Lake Road.

Author's collection

Harper's Gate c1921. A view of the Station Hotel with a horse and cart delivering milk churns to the station.

Author's collection

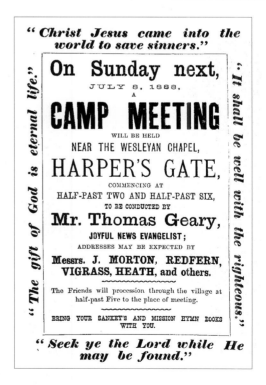

Notices for meetings at the former Wesleyan Chapel at Harper's Gate, which can be seen today behind Camrose Hall. This chapel opened in 1862 and closed in 1912.

Derek Bowcock collection

The start of Lake Road c1904. Facing the Jubilee Stone can be seen the roof of the cobbler's workshop. The first four houses were built on plots of land sold in the 1880 auction. In the background can be seen Albury House and Sylvian House, built on land sold in the 1890 auction. *Author's collection*

Looking up Whorrocks Bank (Horton Road) c1902 with two young girls posing on the Jubilee Stone, which was erected for Queen Victoria's Diamond Jubilee on 20 June 1897. By 1902 the stone also contained the date of her death - 22 January 1901 - and the start of the Boer War on 11 October 1899 and its end on 1 June 1902. The two properties beyond Rose Cottage and Vine Cottage are both called Fern Cottage and were built by 1884. *Author's collection*

The same view in 1920. On the right is the recently built Post Office, replacing the one located in the demolished 18th century property. Infilling of vacant land had taken place following the 1910 auction, with the Wesleyan Chapel, Glenwood and Wynforde. *Author's collection*

1900s view of Vine Cottage and Rose Cottage on Lake Road. Above the door of Rose Cottage is the name of D Bowyer, builder, carpenter and undertaker. *The late Alan Winkle collection*

The 1912 Weslyan Chapel on Lake Road, replacing the earlier Chapel behind Camrose Hall at Harper's Gate. It opened in October 1912.   *Author's collection*

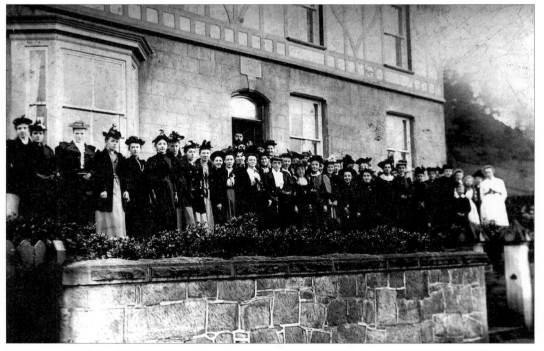

Pine Cottage on Lake Road, built in 1892, with a women's group outside.   *Author's collection*

The Limes Café, situate just off Lake Road, between Wynforde and Albury House, was the first purpose built café in Rudyard. It was opened by James and Emily Guilliard in 1906.

Left: 1950s advertising card for the Limes Café

Guilliard family collection

Albury House c1905, a typical family house on Lake Road, built in 1896 and occupied by Francis Salt. Albury House was in use as a tea room for more than 40 years. Notices advertising "Teas" can be seen on the windows of both front rooms, while the sign to the right of the "lean-to", which was used for teas and cycle storage, reads "Every Accommodation for Cyclists". From c1936 until the late 1950s Fred Abberley ran a mobile grocery business from the house. In the background is Sylvian House, built in 1893. *Author's collection*

A view taken c1908 from Horton Road, looking down on Lake Road and with the station and disused quarry in the background. Sylvian House can be seen. The single storey building in the centre is The Limes Café. and the large house to the right is Nab Wood.   *Author's collection*

British and Foreign Bible Society.
RUDYARD BRANCH.

A MEETING

WILL BE HELD ON
THURSDAY, November 12th, 1903,
IN
Mr. F. SALT'S Large Room.

Rev. J. ALSTON, B.A.,
District Secretary, Shrewsbury,
WILL DELIVER AN ADDRESS ON
'All over the World with the Bible'
Illustrated with Views by Oxy-hydrogen Lantern.

The Chair will be taken at 7-30 p.m., by
Rev. B. BLAKEWAY,
Vicar of Horton.

A COLLECTION in aid of the Funds of the British and Foreign Bible Society.

Your presence and help are earnestly invited.

W. H. JOHNSON, TYP., LEEK.

BRITISH & FOREIGN
BIBLE SOCIETY,
HORTON AND RUDYARD BRANCH.

THE ANNUAL
MEETING
WILL BE HELD IN
Mr. F. SALT'S LARGE ROOM,
ON
Monday, Nov. 20th, 1905.

Rev. R. B. ROBSON, M.A.,
(Deputation) Vicar of St. Pauls, West Bromwich, & Hon.
County Sec. for South Staffordshire, will give an address

"THE BIBLE IN BENGAL"
Illustrated with Views by Oxy-hydrogen Lantern.

Chair to be taken at 7-30 p.m., by
REV. B. BLAKEWAY, M.A.,
VICAR OF HORTON.

A Collection in aid of the Funds of the British and Foreign Bible Society.

Your presence and help are earnestly invited.

W. H. JOHNSON, PRINTER, LEEK.

Notices of prayer meetings to be held at Albury House.

Derek Bowcock collection

One of the more substantial buildings on Lake Road was Underwood, with the original construction on the left dating back to the 18th century.
Author's collection

Celebratory bunting adorns The Beeches on Lake Road in 1910
.Author's collection

Lake Road under snow 1909. A group of four houses can be seen on the left, known then as The Beeches. These large houses were built in the late 1890s and were used from the outset and over succeeding years to provide holiday accommodation and refreshments.

Author's collection

The same view in the early 1950s. Note the signs for Woodside Café and for the Hotel Rudyard car park.

Cooper family collection

The changing face of the Hotel Rudyard. Left is an 1868 view taken from the feeder, with the original water bailiff's house in the foreground and a later extension behind. Above is a typical 1905 Nithsdale postcard of the front of the Hotel Rudyard before the 1906/07 enlargement, which added a floor. Below is a 1907 view with the recently built additional top storey clearly visible.

Author's collection

Looking down from Horton Road over the rooftops of Lake Road and the Hotel Rudyard 1920.

Author's collection

1960s view of the Hotel Rudyard. The sign on the wall says "To the Dining Room".

Ron Lloyd collection

Views of Woodside Café, originally based in one of the houses known as The Beeches.

Top, the tea room pavilion, built in the early 1920s by Georgina Coxon, with an attractive garden. Centre is the entrance to the pavilion and right, the interior.

Author's collection

The NSR purchased swans for the Lake, seen here at the Dam c1908.

Author's collection

Taking the plunge at the Dam in 1924. The landing stage owned by John Hall is in the foreground. In the background at the end of the Dam is the small café run by the Brookes family.   *Author's collection*

A view c1905 from the bay at the south end of the lake, looking towards the Dam in the background. On the left is the Earl of Macclesfield's boathouse.

Author's collection

A view from the same place looking north, with a typical wintry scene of skating by moonlight.

Author's collection

Prior to the 1904 Act the use of the lake for boating was severely restricted to those who owned or leased land on the banks of the lake. After 1904 there was a significant increase in commercial activity on the lake.

Author's collection

A delightful Edwardian scene c1908 at the bay.

Author's collection

1907, rowing and sailing near the Lady of the Lake boathouse.

The late Alan Winkle collection

Sailing up the Lake 1904.

Author's collection

The freezing conditions on the Lake are captured in this Edwardian postcard.   *Author's collection*

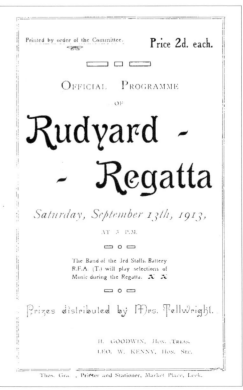

July 1909 bill board from the Manchester Evening Chronicle.   *Author's collection*

1913 Regatta programme.   *Author's collection*

1908 Advertisments   *Leek Post & Times*

Mary Heath (née Austin), on the right, who developed Spite Hall, with Marion Heath in the woodland.
Derek Bowcock collection

Seen here c1896, Fairview was the first major estate to be developed at Rudyard. It was built in 1879/80 by John Munro, a Hanley-based wines and spirits merchant.

Author's collection

Haymaking by the Heath family c1900.
Author's collection

1902 invitation card

Derek Bowcock collection

Below: Arthur Malkin & Sons shearing sheep at Fairboroughs Farm, near Rudyard.

Author's collection

The Jubilee stone being measured at the quarry on the Horton Road in 1897 before its removal to Lake Road.
Author's collection

Stephen Chesters-Thompson was a prominent Manchester brewer and Conservative politican, who only lived in Rudyard from 1890 to 1894; he over-reached himself financially and sold Horton Lodge and the boathouse in 1894 at an enormous financial loss. *Author's collection*

Horton Lodge shortly after it was built by Stephen Chesters-Thompson in 1890. Note the new fencing and recently planted trees. *Author's collection*

Horton Lodge became a Miners' Convalescent Home in 1925, when this photograph was taken.
Author's collection

A later view showing the extension to the Miners' Convalescent Home; after nationalisation in 1948 the Home became an adult education college for two years before it was turned into a Special School for delicate children in 1950.

Author's collection

Superintendent John Cooper and Matron Minnie Cooper with the nursing staff c1925.

Author's collection

Facilities at the Convalescent Home included Bowls and Tennis.

Author's collection

Seen here in the 1930s, Horton Parish Church traces its origins back to the 15th century. *Author's collection*

Seen here in the 1920s, Horton Hall, dating from 1338 is one of the oldest surviving properties in the area
Author's collection.

St Gabriel's Church c1906, as originally built, on the east side of Horton Road.   *Author's collection*

Harpur's Gate, Rudyard.

THE CORNER STONE

of the Building to be hereafter dedicated as a Place of Divine Worship in this portion of the Parish of Horton

✠ WILL BE LAID

On Thursday, June 25th, 1903,

BY

MRS. HUGO SLEIGH, OF LEEK.

The Ceremony will commence at 3-30.

Offerings towards the completion of the work are earnestly solicited, and after Collection will be placed upon the Stone. The sum of £300 is still required.

TEA AND LIGHT REFRESHMENTS
(Admission by Ticket) will be provided near the Site at a charge of Sixpence.

Derek Bowcock collection

St Gabriel's Church c1910, as extended. Built on a steep bank the church suffered from subsidence, ceasing as a place of worship in 1928.   *Alice Boulton collection*

Rudyard Kipling derived his first name from Rudyard Lake, where his parents spent many happy hours. Father John Lockwood Kipling is seen here with his now famous son c1890.

Author's collection.

A portrait c1835, of Fanny Bostock. She inherited Cliffe Park Hall in 1831 following the death of her first cousin and lover, John Haworth. She fought a five year battle in the High Court against the NSR from 1851 to 1856 and was ultimately successful in securing a permanent injunction which prevented the Railway Company from using the Lake for commercial advantage. It took an Act of Parliament in 1904 to overturn this state of affairs.

Christine Chester collection

The Heath family farming at Horton c1905.
Author's collection

Rudyard Féte c1905 in front of the
Jubilee Stone.
The late George Bowyer collection

Hotel Rudyard lawn 1905, with Sylvian House in the background.

Courtesy of Geoffrey Fisher

Hotel Rudyard lawn 1905.

Author's collection

Lakeside path to the north of the Dam on the western side of the lake.

The late Alan Winkle collection

1909 Advertisment for the roller skating rink at Rudyard. *Leek Post & Times*

The new walkway along the west bank

The late Alan Winkle collection

The lake walk on the eastern bank.

Author's collection

The popularity of Rudyard as a holiday destination is clearly reflected in this 1920s view of wooden chalets, looking west above Reacliffe Road. Some of these buildings still survive in their original condition, others have been renovated, but most have been destroyed.

Author's collection

Wits End, on the Horton Road, was built by Frank Ball in 1946 on a plot of land offered for sale in 1885. The stone used was reclaimed from the derelict St Gabriel's Church.

The late Frank Ball

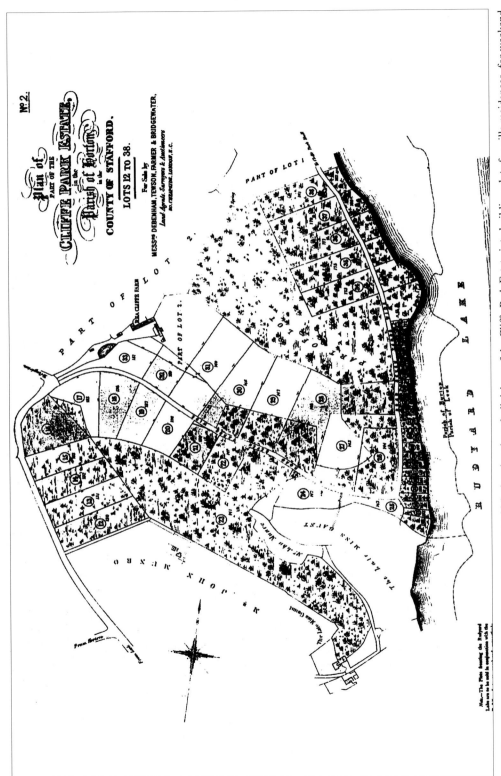

Extract from the auction catalogue of 13 August 1885, showing the sub-divisions of the Cliffe Park Estate into building plots for villa residences, for weekend chalets and for boathouses. ☐The breaking up of the estate in this manner determined the pattern of land ownership and usage down to the present day.
Christine Chester collection

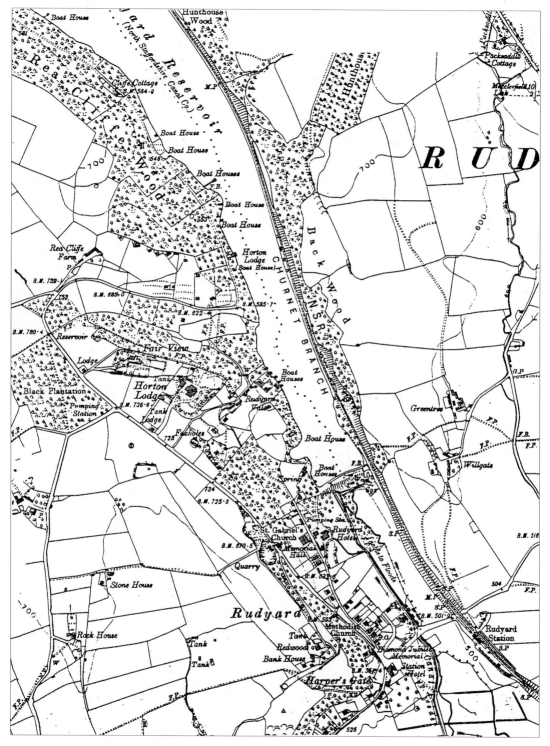

1926 Ordnance Survey map of the southern end of Rudyard Lake, showing the growth of boathouses on the western side.
Crown copyright

The Carriage Drive heading north beyond the Sailing Club towards Cliffe Park Hall.

1940s Youth Hostel Association sign for Cliffe Park Hall. *Author's collection*

Lake Pavilion overlooking the bay at the south end of the lake. Built by the NSR in 1907/08 and let to John Hall, it was managed by Mrs Hall, who can be seen on the left. It was burnt down in 1928. *Author's collection*

St Elmo's Chalet at the side of Spite Hall c1905, with members of the Hammersley family from Leek.

Author's collection

The chalets at various points around the Lake were very popular with working people from the Leek area. They would come for weekend angling and rowing.

Knowles family collection

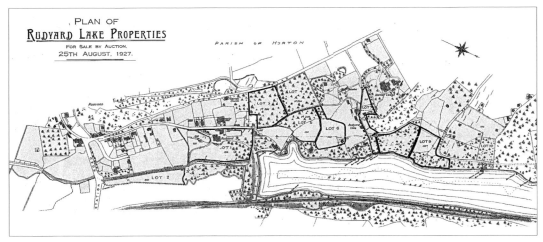

Plan from the auction catalogue of August 1927 for the sale of property owned by the London, Midland and Scottish Railway. This auction saw the sale of the Hotel Rudyard, originally developed from 1851 onwards.

Frank Sutton collection

Part of the 1926 Six Days International Time Trials took place in the Peak District. Some of the riders are seen here passing through Harper's Gate in front of the Station Hotel.

Alice Boulton collection

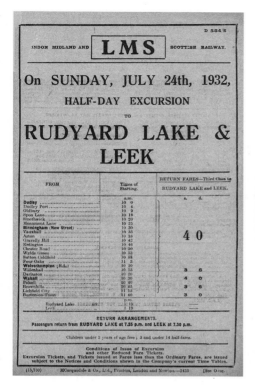

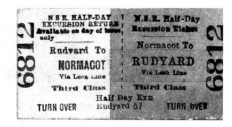

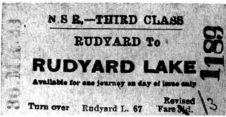

Author's collection

A typical early 1930s local stopping train near Rudyard with a former NSR 4-2-4 K Class locomotive, now LMS No 2185, at the head of a two-coach set. *The late Gordon Walwyn collection*

The lakeside stall of the Sandeman family in the early 1920s.

The late Alan Winkle collection

The newly established Sea Scouts seen here near the site of the ailing Club c1938. Moreton's cottage, the Sea Scouts' headquarters, can be seen in the background.   *Jim Ridgway collection*

PLEASE RETAIN THIS BILL FOR REFERENCE. D 699

LMS

ALTON TOWERS AND GARDENS
The Fairyland of England
Formerly one of the Ducal Homes of England.   Cost over £1,000,000.

On SUNDAY, JULY 15th, 1934

HALF-DAY EXCURSION to

ALTON (for Alton Towers)

RUDYARD LAKE and LEEK

FROM	Times of Starting.	RETURN FARES (Third Class) Alton.	RETURN FARES (Third Class) Rudyard Lake and Leek.
	a.m.	s. d.	s. d.
STECHFORD	10 48	4 L 6	4 0
ASTON	10 55		
GRAVELLY HILL	10 58		
ERDINGTON	11 0		
CHESTER ROAD	11 5		
WYLDE GREEN	11 8	3 6	
SUTTON COLDFIELD	11 12		
FOUR OAKS	11 15		
WOLVERHAMPTON (H.L.)	10 25		
WILLENHALL	10 35		3 6
DARLASTON	10 40		
WALSALL	10 50		4 0
PELSALL	11 3		
BROWNHILLS	11 10	3 0	3 6
LICHFIELD CITY	11 35		
	p.m.		
BURTON	12 2	2 0	3 0

Times of Arrival		12 45 p.m.	Rudyard Lake. 1 10 p.m.	Leek. 1 5 p.m.

Passengers return on day of issue only as follows :— RETURN TIMES ... Depart ...	p.m. 8 5	p.m. 7 40	p.m. 7 44

Arrives STECHFORD 10.20 p.m., WOLVERHAMPTON 10.25 p.m.
L. Fare, Stechford to Leek 4/-.

Children under 3 years of age free ; 3 years and under 14 h...

FOR NOTES, ETC., SEE OTHER SIDE.

7,500 11., 100 P.   Bemrose & Sons Ltd., Derby and London

L.M. & S.R.   FOR CONDITIONS SEE BACK
FISHING TICKET
Entitling holder to Fish in RUDYARD LAKE with Rod & Line from a boat or from the Railway side of the Lake, between the Dam Head and 21½ Mile Post, or from the Dam Head, on the date stamped hereon.
THIS TICKET TO BE DESTROYED AT THE CLOSE OF THE DAY'S FISHING
C. G. ROSE
(District Engineer)
CHARGE 1/-   2667

28 JUL 24   8125

Issued subject to the conditions & regulations in the Cos Time Tables Books Bills & Notices & in the Railway Cos Book of regulations relating to traffic by Passenger Train or other similar service. NOT TRANSFERABLE

EACH SATURDAY and SUNDAY
until 13th September 1952
TO

LEEK   RUDYARD LAKE
CLIFFE PARK and RUSHTON

FROM	DEPART Saturday	DEPART Sunday	THIRD CLASS RETURN FARES Leek	Rudyard Lake	Cliffe Park	Rushton
	p m	p m	s d	s d	s d	s d
STOKE-ON-TRENT	12 55	2 5	1 7	1 10	2 1	2 2
FENTON MANOR	12 57	2 7	1 5	1 8	2 0	2 1
BUCKNALL	1 2	2 12	1 4	1 6	1 9	1 11
MILTON	1 7	2 17	1 1	1 4	1 6	1 8
STOCKTON BROOK	1 12	2 22	11	1 1	1 4	1 5
ENDON	1 15	2 25	10	1 0	1 3	1 4
WALL GRANGE	1 20	2 30	6	10	1 0	1 1
LEEK	1 30	2 40	—	5	9	10

ARRIVAL TIMES	Saturday		p m 1 27	p m 1 33	p m 1 39	p m 1 43
	Sunday		2 38	2 43	2 49	2 52

Passengers return on day of issue of ticket only	Saturday		7 40	7 32	7 26	7 25
	Sunday		7 55	7 47	7 41	7 40

CONDITIONS OF ISSUE OF EXCURSION AND OTHER TICKETS AT LESS THAN ORDINARY FARES

Day, Half-Day and Evening tickets are issued subject to the conditions applicable to tickets of these descriptions as shown in the Bye-Laws and Regulations, General Notices, Regulations and Conditions exhibited at Stations, or where not so exhibited, copies can be obtained free of charge at the Station Booking Office. For luggage allowances also see these Regulations and Conditions.

Children under three years of age, free ; three years and under fourteen, half-fares
TICKETS CAN BE OBTAINED IN ADVANCE AT STATIONS AND AGENCIES
Further information will be supplied on application to Stations, Agencies, or to
Mr. H. BULLOUGH, District Commercial Superintendent, Stoke-on-Trent.
Telephone: Stoke-on-Trent 44121, Extension 26.

June 1952   BR 35002

BRITISH RAILWAYS

Jowett & Sowry, Ltd., Leeds, 1   N 415

Author's collection

Near Cliffe Park station, tracklifting is taking place on the 3 June 1965, with British Railways 2-6-0 locomotive 43115 working the tracklifting train.
Christine Chester collection

Bicentennial Dinner
to celebrate

RUDYARD LAKE
1797-1997

Rudyard Lake Hotel
at 8pm
Thursday March 27 1997

The Rudyard Lake Sailing Club in
the late 1980s.
courtesy Rudyard Lake Sailing Club

Sam Singer and Sam Mansell, who
rowed the lake every Sunday for over
50 years, seen here on 7 April 1996
cutting the tape to inaugurate the new
landing stage. The steamboat is in the
background.

Leek Post & Times

An 1890 Bullock photograph of the snow covered Dam, issued as a postcard in 1902.

The late George Bowyer collection

The same view is captured in this 1906 Sandeman postcard. Note the replacement fencing and the bric-à-brac stall.   *Author's collection*

POSTCARDS

The debt of the local historian to postcard publishers cannot be overstated - their work provides the backbone for historians attempting to capture, for example, the social, industrial or transport scenes in the early years of the twentieth century. The history of postcard publishing is fascinating, but specific to this book, the change in Post Office Regulations that occurred in January 1902 had a dynamic effect on publishing; before that these regulations forbade any message being written other than on the face, together with a view. This limited the attraction of the postcard as a means of communication.

On the relaxation of this regulation the postcard rapidly gained favour, as it had done years earlier on the Continent. Not only were cards sent, as of now, but they were also retained, to a large extent, being one of the Edwardian collecting crazes. In 1907 some 800 million cards were sent in that year alone. The collecting craze was diminished by the outbreak of the First World War in 1914, but postcard publishing continues down to the present day.

In the context of this history of Rudyard, who have been the principal publishers, and what have they published? William Sandeman was probably the doyen of local publishers and his photographs were published by him, and by his family after his death in 1928, for a period from 1903 into the 1930s.

Sandeman was born in 1853 in Scotland, opening a photographic studio at 3, Ball Haye Street, Leek, in April 1884, in partnership with a Mr Hodgson; in 1896 he moved to Greenlands, in Dunwood Lane, Rudyard, and this part of the village is still known as 'Sandeman's Corner'. He closed his Leek studio at the beginning of 1904 and opened a store in Rudyard selling souvenirs, Rudyard Rock and fancy goods of all kinds, including postcards. Sandeman photographed Rudyard and the Lake from the time he arrived in the village in 1896, and it appears that some of his early photographs appeared on his postcards published from 1903 onwards. A small number of the glass plates used for his postcard publishing have still survived.

Another prolific postcard publisher of the Rudyard scene, especially of the Lake when frozen, was George Hill, printer and stationer, who around 1880 set up in business at 8 Stanley Street, Leek. In the 1890s he was joined by his two sons, John and William, and in 1904 the name of the firm was changed to George Hill & Sons. Late in 1902 the firm produced their first postcards for sale in the shop, but the views on the postcards were small; it was not until early in 1904 that the firm produced full sized photographic views. In 1908 the title of the view appeared on the card in capital letters, and postcards published with the descriptions in 'lower case' date from 1918/25.

A major publisher of Rudyard postcards was the North Staffordshire Railway, which, like other Railway companies at the time, produced 'official' postcards to encourage passenger travel on their own networks, and to appeal to the collector. The NSR produced a series of 6-card sets covering Rudyard scenes and these were sold in envelopes for 3d each. They were promoted by the NSR in descriptive booklets. Set 1 was published by May 1905, Set 5 in May 1906, Set 8 by August 1907, Set 15 by July 1909 and Set 23 by August 1914.

William Shaw of Burslem was another prolific postcard publisher starting in 1905 and adding to his business of wholesale stationery, toy and fancy goods merchant. He published scenes of Staffordshire, Cheshire and Derbyshire and there were several series covering Rudyard; he acquired and commissioned negatives from local photographers.

The oldest photographs to appear on postcards were those published by the Bullock Brothers of Macclesfield. This business was established c1849 on Hibel Road, Macclesfield adjacent to the new railway station. There are many instances of photographs taken in 1890 appearing on postcards from 1902 onwards - skating scenes and boating views in particular, with a young boy with starched collar and black cap in the pictures, featuring in older photographs.

Harry Breaks arrived in Leek from Nottingham c1920. He established a bazaar in Leek and from 1921 started publishing several series of postcards. He had a stall on the Dam, from which he ran a linked business of snapping tourists. In the mid 1930s he opened an open air swimming pool at Freshwater, on the main Macclesfield road.

Local events provided further material for the local photographer and postcard publisher; within a few days of some topical event a run of two or three hundred relevant postcards would be on sale in the locality. For example, as featured in this book, the opening of the Roller Skating Rink in 1909, the laying of the Foundation Stone for the new Methodist Chapel in 1912, and the numerous regattas are all typical of the events captured on camera on behalf of the local postcard publisher.

Postcards of Rudyard published throughout the Edwardian era are particularly interesting because they capture the physical changes that took place between 1900 and 1915, such as the landing stages, the Dam, the boat houses, the Hotel Rudyard, the railway station, the 18th century houses at the start of Lake Road and the golf course.

Some local traders published their own postcards - Bentley, the landlord of the Station Hotel c1908; George Heath, the boat operator 1906; Mary Heath, owner of Spite Hall café and restaurant c1905; George Henshall, official photographer to Hotel Rudyard c1912, Tommy Stone, who owned Kingswood Store, c1923 and Harry Breaks, who owned the Freshwater open air swimming pool. R A Publishing produced sets of 6 cards for the Woodside Café from the early 1920s.

National publishers producing Rudyard cards up to 1920 included Boots, WH Smith, Valentine & Sons, Doncaster Roto Photo.

Other local postcard publishers included E E Heathcote of Moorfields, Leek (using photographs taken by W H Nithsdale in 1905), W H Eaton of Derby Street, Leek, and J Wood of Milton (mid 1920s). An interesting set of postcards, using early views, was published by Frank Amor, of Alsager, from c1903 under the name of the "Roma" series. Lilywhite of Halifax published several series of postcards from 1923.

More recent postcard publishers include Francis Frith & Co (late 1960s); J Salmon in the late 1960s and 1970s; E T W Dennis & Sons Ltd (1980s), J/V Postcards (1980s), the Staffordshire Federation of Women's Institutes (1985 onwards) and the Staffordshire Moorlands District Council (1987).

A 1902 Hill view which shows the Dam before the water level of the lake was raised.

Author's collection

The same view in this 1906 Hill postcard, shows the raised Dam wall and the recently installed landing stage.

Author's collection

Two views by the same unknown postcard publisher, of the east and west shoreline c1902, before the commercialisation began to develop from 1905 onwards.

Top: *Unwin family collection*
Bottom: *Author's collection*

A 1905 view, taken from the old quarry, of the station platform in the foreground and the housing along Lake Road in the background. *Author's collection*

THE VILLAGE — RUDYARD.

The same view in this 1920s Breaks postcard, showing the 1911 lengthening of the platform and the 1911/1912 developments on Lake Road of the Chapel and the adjacent houses.

Author's collection

An early Hill postcard dated 1902, of boys walking along the edge of the lake towards the Dam.

Author's collection

1908 Advertising card for the Station Hotel.

Author's collection

Advertising card published by George Henshall of Macclesfield c1912 for the Hotel Rudyard and the boating business of George Heath. *Author's collection*

1945 advertising card published by the Youth Hostels Association.   *Author's collection*

1902 Advertising card for manures.

Author's collection

A 1909 'event' card published by Hill, showing the interior of the roller skating rink. It was located on land behind the 1922 Memorial Institute.   *The late George Bowyer collection*

A 1907 'event' card published by Sandeman of a Gala Day .

Author's collection

Laying Memorial Stones, New Wesleyan Church, Rudyard, April 25th, 1912.

An 'event' card, published at the end of April 1912, to commemorate the laying of the foundation stones for the Wesleyan Chapel.

Author's collection

Envelope used by the NSR to sell sets of six 'official' postcards.

Author's collection

Plane crash in the 1920s in Rudyard woods. PC Jackson can be seen centre left.

The late George Bowyer collection

One of the delightful set of NSR 'official' postcards published in July 1909, and promoting the Golf Club. The two boats seen here are moored at Hall's landing stage. *Author's collection*

This postcard by J Wood of Milton captures a view of the Dam from in front of the water bailiff's house in the mid 1920s. Note the advertisement for Photocharm on the side of the valve house. Also the advert for Cadbury's chocolate on the wooden hut in the foreground.

Author's collection

This 1920s postcard records the Leek Tandem cycling club during a visit to Rudyard.

Author's collection

During the 1920s and 1930s 'event' cards were published of the Rudyard Christmas pantomimes and of fancy dress dances.

Author's collection

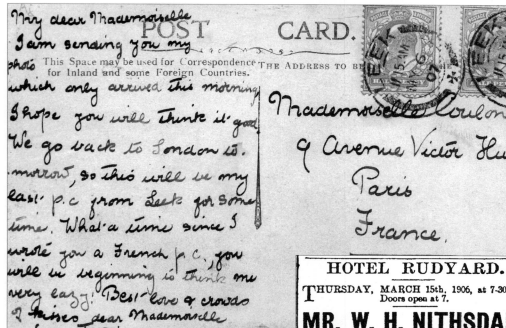

My dear Mademoiselle
I am sending you my
photo. This Space may be used for Correspondence
for Inland and some Foreign Countries.
which only arrived this morning
I hope you will think it good
We go back to London to-
morrow, so this will be my
last p.c from Leek for some
time. What a time since I
wrote you a French p.c. you
will be beginning to think me
very lazy! Best love & crowds
of kisses dear Mademoiselle
from Jessie

POST CARD.

THE ADDRESS TO BE

Mademoiselle Coulon
9 Avenue Victor Hugo
Paris
France.

HOTEL RUDYARD.

THURSDAY, MARCH 15th, 1906, at 7-30 p.m.
Doors open at 7.

MR. W. H. NITHSDALE

WILL PRESENT HIS LIME-LIGHT

"GLIMPSES OF NORTH STAFFORD."

Vocalist: Mr. ERNEST RUSHTON.

First Seats, One Shilling; Second Seats, Sixpence;
Children at half-prices. Carriages at 9-45 p.m.
A Brake will run from Flower's Livery Stables,
Shoobridge street, Leek, at 6-45 p.m. Fare 6d.
return.

W H Nithsdale was a photographer and writer who published an illustrated guide to the Highlands of Staffordshire in 1905. He was usually accompanied by his niece Jessie, who also took photographs and this Hill postcard, which would seem to be of one of her own photographs, was sent by her in May 1907.

Author's collection

Early 1920s view of the Rudyard Ladies Football team, publisher unknown.

Derek Bowcock collection

Rudyard Lake.

A Hill postcard published c1920, with a view taken looking down from above the Carriage Drive just south of Cliffe Park Hall.

Author's collection

This Francis Frith late 1960s postcard shows the 1870s boathouse and the boat hiring business being operated, by this time, by the Maynard family. One of the former lifeboats can be seen moored at the landing stage.

Author's collection

An early 1960s J Salmon postcard of the north end of the lake.

Author's collection

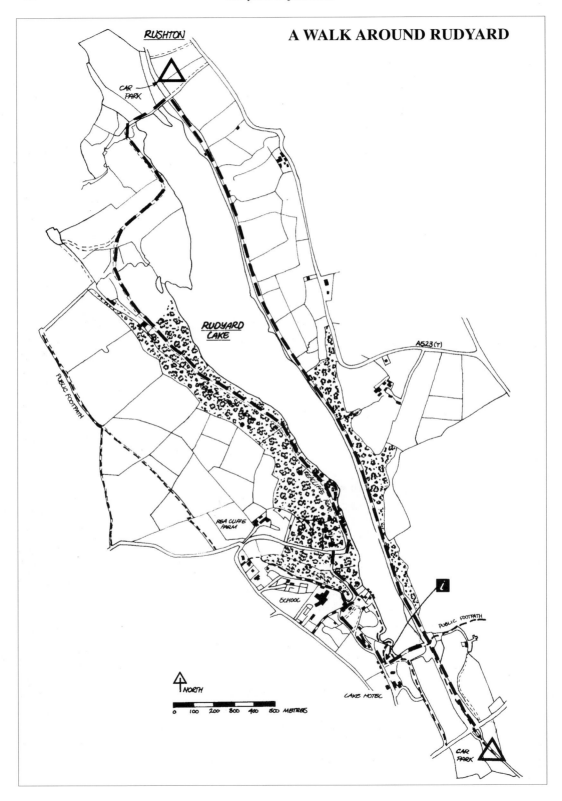

A WALK AROUND RUDYARD

RUSHTON

CAR PARK

RUDYARD LAKE

PUBLIC FOOTPATH

A523 (T)

REA CLIFFE FARM

SCHOOL

PUBLIC FOOTPATH

LAKE HOTEL

CAR PARK

NORTH

0　100　200　300　400　500 METRES

A WALK AROUND RUDYARD

Station Car Park

Parking your car or abandoning your bicycle to set out from the car park which now exists on the site of the former Rudyard Station, it is hard to imagine that this was once a small country station built to serve a small country parish, providing the villagers with access to the markets of Leek and Macclesfield, to a school in Leek and enabling them to commute to the Potteries and for local farmers to despatch their milk to distant Manchester and London.

The station opened in July 1850 and from its early years was having to cope with large numbers of visitors, attracted by special events or visiting on bank holidays and wakes weeks. Even though there were improvements made to the station facilities between 1899 and 1911, they had made little impact on the large numbers using the station. Almost every year between 1904 and 1913, between eight and twelve thousand visitors arrived during the Stoke Wakes. During special events, such as trade union rallies and the like, the numbers coming by rail were anything between six and thirteen thousand. This was in addition to visitors from Leek, who would walk along the Feeder.

Looking down the car park towards Harper's Gate, the land to the right of the road was originally part of the NSR estate, which passed to the London, Midland & Scottish Railway on 'grouping' in 1923 and, together with several other properties, including Hotel Rudyard, was sold on 25 August 1927. The pair of semi-detached houses was built in 1929 along with Rudyard Garage. The feeder to Leek passes under the road and, just before that, on the garage parking area, is the site of the Earl of Macclesfield's estate yard. also sold off in 1927. Looking along the feeder to the right you see Winshaw Knoll, built by John Brealey on a site that comprised four lots in the 1890 Auction. Beyond stands the Hotel Rudyard, developed from out of the original Water Bailiff's house from 1851.

The Dam

Standing on the Dam and looking up the Lake, with a handful of people walking past, it is now hard to envisage the teeming masses who walked there over the decades from the early 1850s down to the 1940s. What you see of the Dam today is as it was rebuilt in the 1905/07 period, with people able to walk over the entire length of the Dam and pass along the bridge over the sluice. Earlier sketches coinciding with the opening of the railway line on 13 July 1849 show the features less square at the Dam; the land owned by the Earl of Macclesfield, on the east side of the Dam, was clearly fenced off from the land on the rest of the Dam, which was owned by the Canal Company.

By around 1900, one or two pushcart stalls began to appear near the slope down from the Hotel Rudyard, but it was not until the commercialisation of the Lake after the passing of the 1904 NSR Act that two or three fixed structures were erected in front of the water bailiff's house. Hand carts also began to appear, including Granelli's ice cream cart from Macclesfield. With the growing popularity of the Lake the number of stalls increased, all selling various forms of bric-à-brac, confectionery and Rudyard Rock.

By the early 1920s stall holders included the Sandemans, the Winkle family, the Guilliards, Harry Breaks and Wilhemina Rodgers; Harry Breaks took photographs and the Podestas, Granelli's (from Macclesfield), El Dorado (from Manchester) and others sold ice cream.

The Dam itself underwent changes c1907/08, with a bandstand (housing a stentaphone) being constructed, together with a wooden dance floor (now concreted over) and a wooden shelter facing it. This remained the position until 1939 and the outbreak of the Second World War. Peacetime saw the arrival of fun fair swings and roundabouts, which survived into the 1960s.

On either side of the Dam, facing each other across the Lake from 1906, were the boat hiring businesses, that of John Hall on the west bank and that of George Heath, on the east bank. George Heath was from an old Horton family and had married Mary Austin, whose mother developed the Spite Hall refreshment facilities and tourist accommodation. In the 1890s George Heath used to row visitors in a small boat, which was stored in one of his boathouses a few hundred yards north of the Dam. From 1906 onwards there was fierce competition between Hall and Heath - Hall renting a landing stage built by the NSR and Heath building steps down from the Dam and having a boat hiring business directly opposite Hall's. Postcards covering a period from 1902 down to the 1920s illustrate the changing features of the site of Hall's and Heath's landing stages - from a time when people would scramble over the stones in 1902 to board a boat, down to 1920 when enlarged and comparatively sophisticated facilities existed for the hundreds of people joining the boats - and the opening by Hall, c1918, of boat building and repairing services. These businesses continued until c1939 and the outbreak of war, after which, from the original Hall landing stage the Maynards restarted the boating business, initially with 60 rowing boats, which lasted until 1969. From 1972 Roy Evett operated the Rudyard Princess as Rudyard Pleasure Boats for about ten years. Whilst private rowing has continued over the years, notably the late Sam Singer and Sam Mansell, who rowed the Lake every Sunday morning for over 50 years, Rudyard Lake Limited has recently reintroduced boats for hire from near the Dam.

Two boathouses can be seen from the Dam, immediately on the left and on the right. The one on the left, now a Visitor Centre, was formally the Trent & Mersey Canal boathouse, built in the late 1870s to replace an earlier boathouse which was located in the bay thirty yards to the north. The boathouse on the right, the Earl of Macclesfield's boathouse, was built between 1849 and 1868; in very recent years it housed the steam boat owned by Roger Lees. The boat is now owned by the Robinson family and there are plans for it to be operated by the local volunteer group, the Rudyard Lake League of Friends.

The two stone towers housed water valves to control the flow of water into the feeder going to Leek and beyond, the original valves being replaced in 1992. A collection of new buildings, the toilet and changing block (2000), the Visitor Centre (2001) and the temporary utilities building (1997) can be seen. Look closely and you will see the Rudyard well, used for well dressing ceremonies in the late 19th century. Climbing up from the Dam you will pass, on the right, the 1852 water bailiff's house, still in use as such and owned by British Waterways.

The left bank

Climbing up from Lake Road, on the right can be seen the Caravan Park in front of Spite Hall. Adjacent to the house stands the former green timbered Spite Hall café and the formerly pebble-dashed timber chalet known as St Elmo's. Also on the right is a small green chalet, Geelong, which was a former refreshment room brought from the north end of the Lake in 1926. Foxholes and a former quarry stand on the higher left hand slope, behind which are the substantial estates of Horton Lodge (1890/91) and Fair View (1879/80). All these properties are visible from across the Lake. Climbing towards Reacliffe Road the occasional wooden weekend chalet, built in the early years of the 20th century, can still be seen, though no longer in use as such. Reaching Reacliffe Road - originally a late 18th century seven yards wide carriage drive from Wolf Dale at the top of the Lake - cross to Horton Road and bearing right, a delightful walk of about ³/₄ mile brings you to the Rudyard Lake Sailing Club.

Along Reacliffe Road you pass a series of entrances to the boathouses, built at various times from c1885 up to the present day. Again, better views are obtained from the opposite bank of the Lake. Each of these boathouses has been built on a very narrow strip of land; this is a direct consequence of the August 1885 decision to auction off the Cliffe Park Estate in 38 lots. Along the top of Reacliffe Road some of the field boundaries correspond to the 1885 building plots, whilst off the Carriage Drive to the right the narrow strips of land again correspond to the building plots. Of particular interest are Lower Horton Lodge (1891 - formerly Horton Lodge Boathouse), Challinor's Boathouse (early 1890s), Fortside (built in the 1930s), Sandy Point (c1914), the Lady of the Lake (1893) - designed by William Sugden and formerly known as Davenport's Boathouse), the Brackens Boathouse (c1900) and the former Bilton's Boathouse, bright green, built c1900.

On the left stands the delightfully maintained early 1900s wooden chalet, The Brackens, now with a modern wooden garage to its left, and originally with its own boathouse down at the lakeside. This formed one of five similar lots offered for sale in 1885. Nearby, on the site of the former Bilton's chalet, a new chalet is being built. A few hundred yards further along lies a narrow stone building. This is Cliffe Park Lodge, built in 1871 as the lodge to Cliffe Park Hall. Directly facing the Lodge is the £750,000 major development scheme of the Rudyard Lake Sailing Club, which was established in 1956.

Following the track as it wends firstly through woodland and then open pasture we arrive at Cliffe Park Hall, now in private ownership. Former owners have included John Haworth, his cousin Fanny Bostock, her nephew Duncan Boothman, the North Staffordshire Railway (who leased it to the Rudyard Lake Golf Club as a residential Club House from 1906 to 1926) and the successor LMS (who leased it to the Youth Hostels Association from 1933 to 1969). It is now in private ownership.

The 18th green of the Golf Club was directly facing the entrance and the 17th green is still visible to the right. Passing the Hall and dropping down towards the Lake, Barnslee Farm, which is around 300 years old, can be seen to the left; purchased in 1904 by the NSR, and always a working farm, it was sold out of railway ownership in 1981. Careful observation still reveals evidence of the former bunkers and tees. At the lakeside, where the path veers to the left, was the site of the original club house and the tea room, where some tourist activities were introduced in the late 1950s.

The top of the lake

Passing through gates we arrive at the north end of the Lake where the survivors of the 1920s weekend chalets can be seen. It was in this area that enemy bombs fell during the Second World War.

We have now reached the top of the Lake, where the feeder comes in from Dane Bridge, and it is here that the dry and nutrient-rich silt has been deposited on the Lake bed.

This has attracted many species of plant life, some quite rare, and has become an area of great attraction to migratory bird life. During times of water draw down in the spring and summer months, mud flats appear. These are attractive to wading birds, particularly during their spring and autumn migrations, when Lapwing, Curlew, Sandpiper, Dunlin and Redshank spend time foraging for invertebrates in the soft mud whilst en route between their upland nesting ground and winter coastal haunts. No fishing or boating is permitted here in order to encourage wildlife development.

The right bank

We now come to the trackbed of the Churnet Valley Railway and the site of the 1905 Rudyard Lake station, renamed Cliffe Park station from 1926, built to encourage tourists to the northern end of the Lake. These were, in the main, anglers, golfers and walkers, there being no boating facilities here. There was a small wooden station on the right, facing south, with waiting shelters on both sides. The station closed on 7 November 1960. The railway line runs straight and parallel to the Lake for just over two miles. It is along this section that angling has been most popular for almost 150 years, and several angling huts can be seen. The most significant building on this section is 'The Ridgway', opened in 1994 after an earlier fire had destroyed the 1992 building; it houses the Sea Scouts, who have been based there since 1936. Here can also be seen a wooden railway hut.

There are excellent views across the Lake. In front of Cliffe Park Hall and Barnslee was the first golf course of 1906; nine holes originally, it was extended to 18 holes in 1908, on land behind Barnslee Farm. It closed in 1926 due to falling numbers, as several wealthy families left the area because of the increase in tourism. Look carefully and you will see a bunker, tee or green. Next into view comes the Sailing Club and then boathouses of all shapes and sizes, and of different eras; the narrow strips of land in which they sit, purchased at the 1885 Auction, are clearly visible. At Hunthouse Wood the 1985 miniature railway has its terminus. Halfway down, the prominent older boathouses of Lady of the Lake, Challinor's (with corrugated iron roof) and Horton Lodge dominate this stretch, with some smaller boathouses such as Fortside (1930s) and Sandy Point (c1914) squeezed in between them. Nearer the Dam are a cluster of three older boathouses, the first two being built around 1900 and the furthest by 1885. Perched above can still be seen Lakeside, a 1900 wooden chalet.

On the bank above the boathouses stands the Caravan Park, whose origins date back to the 1950s, with Spite Hall and Rudyard Villa, both built in the early 1860s, also visible. Approaching the Dam there is a small bay just north of the café; this was the site of the original Trent & Mersey Canal boathouse. Above it, tucked away in the woods, was a café built by the NSR and let to John Hall. This café flourished from 1908 to 1928. The boathouse on the Dam has been converted during 2000/2001 from the mid-1870s boathouse of the Trent & Mersey Canal Company.

Rudyard Lake station in the 1950s, looking north from what is now the car park. The small goods shed, centre left, was built in 1901. *Author's collection*

Rudyard station 1908, a view from the disued quarry above the station, looking north. With a substantial increase in the numbers of tourists, the station underwent some modest alterations in the early 1900s, with a new waiting shelter being erected. The name was changed in April 1926 to Rudyard Lake station. It closed on 7 November 1960. *Author's collection*

Rudyard Lake station 1970, awaiting demolition. It was built in the half timbered plastered style in 1850. The signal box is just visible in the background.   *Author's collection*

Rudyard Lake station in the late 1950s, looking south with a typical three-coach train on the Churnet route from Uttoxeter to Macclesfield. The locomotive is Fowler 2-6-4T No 42315 off Macclesfield locomotive shed. Note the nameboard on the signal box, "Rudyard Station", even though the station was renamed Rudyard Lake in April 1926.   *Author's collection*

The approach to the station in 1920. The stone warehouse is in the centre of this Doncaster Roto Photo postcard. *The late George Bowyer collection*

A view from the railway bridge c1906, looking towards Harper's Gate. The workshops for the Earl of Macclesfield's estate, now Frank Sutton's garage, can be seen in the foreground, immediately beyond which is the feeder to Leek, with a stone bridge to the right. The Knoll, overlooking the feeder, dominates the skyline to the right. *Author's collection*

Abberley's Garage in the early 1950s. It was built by Tom Brookes in 1929 on land sold by the LMS in 1927, and taken over by John Abberley in 1936.

Frank Sutton collection

Two views of Harper's Gate from the station platform. Top is a Bullock postcard dating back to 1896 and shows the recently planted garden of The Knoll in the foreground. Centre is Holly Bank, 1891, now known as Camrose Hall. The bottom Sandeman postcard c1900, shows several of the 1890s houses on Lake Road, with the black and white timbered Pine Cottage clearly visible.   *The late George Bowyer collection*

A delightful view of the Rudyard Tennis Club celebrating its formation c1922. It was located in the field to the right of the railway line, just beyond the bridge.   *Derek Bowcock collection*

This is a delightful 1900s view of Hotel Rudyard, with the path to the Hotel winding up from the feeder, the route of which can be seen in the foreground.   *Author's collection*

The sluice on the east side of the Dam c1920. The railway line is just visible bottom left. The footbridge (1905) and the wooden dance floor (1908) can be seen beyond the trees.   *Author's collection*

Ivan Nixon, the popular water bailiff for many years, seen here c1959 working at the sluice. Beyond the wooden fence is a platelayer's hut built by the NSR.   *Author's collection*

Members of the Brookes and Walker families in the late 1920s, on the east side of the Dam. In the background is the refreshment kiosk operated by the Brookes family of Willgate Farm.

Brookes family collection

A delightful Edwardian view looking through the Arch hedge, most of which still survives.

Author's collection

1868 view of the Earl of Macclesfield's boathouse This is the earliest surviving picture of the Dam.

Author's collection

A typical view c1909 of the enormous crowds flocking to the Dam during the Edwardian era. Note the new bandstand on the right.   *Author's collection*

On the east bank - a typical Edwardian rowing scene, with Heath's boating facilities on the right.
                                                                          Author's collection

A promotional postcard c1910 published for George Heath, with his boat 'Grace Darling' in the foreground. Note the steps leading down from the Dam to his motor boat, a method of descent which only lasted a few years.   *Author's collection*

Some of George Heath's rowing boats c1910.

Author's collection

An 1890 view taken by Bullock and published as a postcard in 1902. The white fencing in the background marks the boundary of the Earl of Macclesfield's estate.   *The late George Bowyer collection*

Another Bullock view, December 1890, and later used for a postcard. The Lake was frozen over for more than two months.   *The late George Bowyer collection*

A similar view along the Dam in 1908. Note the wooden stall on the right. *Author's collection*

The west side of the Dam c1902, showing the dirty and neglected nature of the foreshore before the later developments made it an attractive boating location. *The late George Bowyer collection*

A 1900 view of ladies rowing at the Dam in front of the Canal Company boathouse.

Author's collection

Edwardian finery on the landing stage c1908.

The late Alan Winkle collection

1910 view of Hall's landing stage, taken from a surviving Sandeman glass plate.

The late Alan Winkle collection

A view from the Dam c1920, with the boat repairing sheds of Hall and Son on the left.

Author's collection

A view of the landing stage c1921 with some of Hall's fleet on parade. Hall started to operate boats with awnings from c1918 with the larger ones seating around 20 people. Three smaller boats, all with awnings and all of different design, can be seen on the right and in background.   *Author's collection*

A view taken from the Lake c1918, looking across to the Hall and Son landing stage. Note the variety of boats, including those with awnings. The steps leading to the left of the boathouse are visible, as is the booking office.   *Author's collection*

Good Friday 1936 and frozen over. *Author's collection*

The landing stage of the boating business operated at the Dam by the Maynard family in the 1950s.
Geoffrey Fisher collection

'Rudyard Queen', one of two former lifeboats purchased from Birkenhead by George Maynard in 1946. The Maynard family ran this boat business until 1969.   *Geoffrey Fisher collection*

Derelict boat belonging to John Hall, seen here in 1936 in the bay at the south end of the lake. The mid and late 1930s saw a decline in the Lake's popularity and the Hall business had ceased by the outbreak of the Second World War in 1939. In the background can be seen 'Geelong', formerly a refreshment room at the north end of the lake, which was dismantled in 1926 and floated down the Lake to be rebuilt at its present site.

Jim Ridgway collection

Climbing from the side of the Lake, a busy scene in 1920.　　　　　*Author's collection*

A 1900 view of the 1852 water bailiff's house.

Author's collection

The Kingswood Bungalow c1923 was built for Tommy Stone. It was a useful village store which also sold bric-à-brac and Rudyard Rock. It was demolished c1986 to be replaced with a house of the same name on its site.   *Author's collection*

1890 view of Lake Road looking towards Harper's Gate, with Red Cottage and Lilac Cottage on the right.
The late George Bowyer collection

A few yards further along, again looking towards Harper's Gate with the Hotel Rudyard beyond the trees on the left. *The late George Bowyer collection*

An 1890 view looking towards the site of the later 1950s municipal housing.

The late George Bowyer collection

Brassington's Café c1930. A view looking north along Lake Road with the entrance to the Hotel Rudyard car park on the right. Arthur Brassington was a water bailiff for many years; he lived at Reservoir House and, as for many locals, the seasonal income from the café was very important.   *The late Ivan Nixon collection*

St Elmos Chalet c1907, with the Hammersley family in front. In its pebbledash form it is just visible from the footpath climbing up with the caravan park on the right.

Author's collection

Rudyard Vale c1896 showing Rudyard Villa on the left and Spite Hall in the centre. Both properties were built in the early 1860s. Bottom left is part of the agricultural smallholding of Foxholes, with part of the quarry crushing plant clearly visible. This postcard is from the 'Roma Series', published in 1903. *Author's collection*

Derek Bowcock collection

Staffordshire County Council.

TECHNICAL INSTRUCTION COMMITTEE.

COURSES OF TEN WEEKLY LESSONS IN

COOKERY

AND IN

Dress-Cutting

WILL BE GIVEN BY

Miss Drury,

AT

SPITE HALL, RUDYARD,

ON FRIDAYS.

FIRST LESSON APRIL 25th, 1902.

| COOKERY | - | - | - | 2-30 to 4-30. |
| DRESS-CUTTING | - | 5-30 to 7-30. |

Names of Pupils desiring to attend the above Class should be sent in at once to—

MRS. BADDELEY, Hon. Sec., Rudyard,

From whom all information may be obtained.

Fee for each Course of 10 Lessons, 2s.; for a Single Lesson, 3d.

THOMAS TURNER,
County Technical Offices,   Director of Technical Instruction.
Stafford, April 15th, 1902.

J. & C. MORT, PRINTERS, STAFFORD.

Camping party outside Spite Hall on the day of a Regatta.

Author's collection

Wedding party at Spite Hall c1905, with all its Edwardian finery.

Author's collection

Spite Hall Tearoom, built c1902.
Derek Bowcock collection

A view from Foxholes in the early
1950s of the Spite Hall caravan site.
Derek Bowcock collection

Two views of the Shady Oaks chalet. Top, the original chalet and bottom, the replacement chalet after the original was burnt down.

Author's collection

The delightful woodland walk climbing above
The Villa and Spite Hall.
The late Alan Winkle collection

An early 1980s view of the restored
'Maidenhill'. In the foreground, right, can be
seen the roof of a small timber chalet on the
edge of the Spite Hall Caravan Site.
Author's collection

Horton Lodge Boathouse was the second of 14 boathouses to be built on the west side of the lake between 1880 and 1925. Built in 1890/91 it is seen here in the early 1980s from Reacliffe Road.

Christine Pemberton

Fortside is a delightful boathouse built by Bill Burdis in the early 1930s.

Burdis family collection

Lady of Lake boathouse c1905 is the largest and most prominent of the Lake's boathouses. It was designed by the well known Leek architect, William Larner Sugden.

Author's collection

The Bracken's boathouse c1905 can be seen in the foreground, one of two built c1900 north of the Lady of Lake; this boathouse still survives.

Author's collection

The Drive c1905, climbing up from the Lady of the Lake boathouse towards Cliffe Park Lodge and the Sailing Club. This postcard was produced by the national publisher J Valentine.   *Author's collection*

A 1920s view of Biltons delightful wooden bungalow, built c1900.

Author's collection

Cliffe Park Lodge built c1871 served as a lodge for Cliffe Park Hall. This is a 1919 view with two week old Reginald Rigby on the knee of a governess.

Rigby family collection

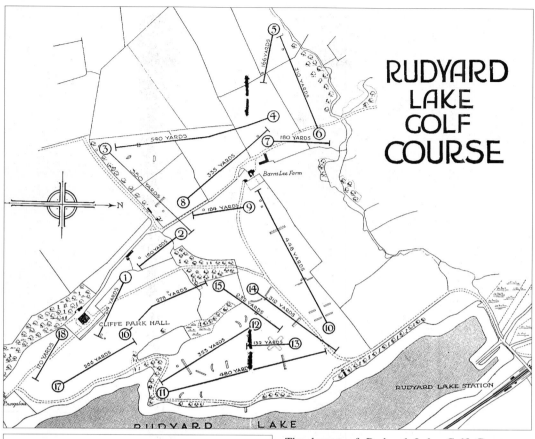

The layout of Rudyard Lake Golf Course, as featured in the 1922 Official Handbook.

Extract from YHA Handbook of Hostels 1937.

Author's collection

LENGTH AND BOGEY OF THE COURSE.

The length and bogey of the holes are as follows :—

	YDS.	BOGEY.		YDS.	BOGEY
1. The Drive	214	4	10. Halfway Hse.	448	5
2. The Dingle	160	3	11. The Lake	480	5
3. Birch Trees	350	5	12. Park Pond	353	4
4. Cloud End	540	5	13. The Spinney	132	3
5. The Caldron	166	3	14. Wolfdale	312	4
6. The Vale	310	5	15. The Croft	232	4
7. Barnslee	180	4	16. Foxholes	278	4
8. Fair View	335	5	17. Paradise	266	4
9. Shutlingslow	184	3	18. Home	179	4
	2439	37		2680	37
				2439	37
				5119	74

Extract from 1922 Handbook.

Author's collection

Cliffe Park Hall was leased to the officers of Rudyard Lake Golf Club. This Hill postcard view c1920 shows the 18th green on the left.

Author's collection

A 1922 view of the green of the 266 yard 17th hole with its panoramic view of the lake; this hole was called 'Paradise'.

Author's collection

Looking north the bunkers in front of the 11th green are clearly visible. At 480 yards the 11th hole was the longest on the course and called 'The Lake'.

Author's collection

This official postcard of the NSR was published in 1906 and shows the interior of the Chalet at the north end of the Lake, which was built by the NSR and leased to Mrs Gale.

Author's collection

This NSR 'official' postcard shows a view looking down toward the Lake from the 1st tee of the original 9-hole golf course. In the background can be seen the original club house in the centre and behind a small refreshment room; both these buildings were built in the spring of 1906, ready for the opening of the course on 19 April 1906. It became an 18-hole course during 1908 and this 1st hole became the 10th hole, playing downhill rather than uphill on the original course. It was 448 yards long, the third longest, and was called Halfway House. *Author's collection*

The NSR, with new powers under the 1904 Act, established several refreshment chalets on the west side of the lake. This particular chalet was moved in 1926 and re-established as a house, now called 'Geelong', facing Spite Hall. *Roy Lewis collection*

Some boating took place at the north end of the lake in the late 1950s.

G Bailey

A typical Edwardian view at the north end of the lake.

Author's collection

North end of the lake in 1905, with a view of the back of Rudyard Lake station. There were no opportunities for boat hire here. Note the newly created paths and freshly painted bench. The Dane feeder comes into the Lake where the Dam sweeps round to the left.

The late George Bowyer collection

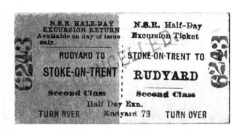

Author's collection

Rudyard Lake station was opened on 1 May 1905 at the north end of the lake to attract tourists, mainly anglers and walkers, but also golfers who would be transported by horse and trap to the Club House. This is a view taken from the former Carriage Drive from Wolfdale Farm to Reacliffe Road. The building was timber framed with a brick chimney. Beyond the station building on the platform is an earth closet or toilet.

Christine Chester collection

A view from the same spot some 55 years later. Whilst the station building is well maintained, the fencing needs some repair. A Uttoxeter to Macclesfield stopping train is about to depart. The station was renamed Cliff Park in April 1926 and became an unmanned 'Halt' in the late 1930s. *Courtesy of the late W Brown*

General View.   — Rudyard Lake Golf Club.

A view across the lake of Cliffe Park Hall, the residential Club House for the Golf Club. Bunkers on the 11th and 12th holes can be seen in the foreground beyond the Lake, and behind is the 16th green. This is a Harry Breaks postcard, published in 1922.   *Roy Lewis collection*

Moreton's cottage c1990 was used as the headquarters of the Stoke-on-Trent 89th Sea Scouts from 1936 until it was replaced in 1992 by the first 'Ridgway'. On the right can be seen a surviving railway hut; off picture to the right is the railway track bed, the track having been lifted in July 1964.   *Jim Ridgway*

The Sea Scouts headquarters 1998, with the second 'Ridgway', built in 1994, to replace the first 'Ridgway' which was burnt down. The railway hut and railway track are in the background.   *Jim Ridgway*

The arrival of the only surviving Tiger Moth seaplane to Rudyard Lake in the summer of 1979. Fully restored, bright red in colour, the little plane spent the entire weekend flying up and down the Lake, landing and taking off from the Sailing Club. Vast crowds turned out to watch, gathering both at the Sailing Club and also massing on the main Leek to Macclesfield Road at the viewing point near the garage. The plane departed early on the Monday morning, flying past the boathouses at balcony level, to the delight of the residents. The Sailing Club headquarters is the low flat building on the left and Cliffe Park Lodge is in the background.

Christine Pemberton

Challinor's boathouse and the Lady of the Lake c1900. Compare this with a view from the same location today, and the large number of boathouses that have been, and are being, developed on the lakeside.

Author's collection

Horton Lodge boathouse in the foreground and Challinor's boathouse in the background c1915. The Horton Lodge boathouse, now known as Lower Horton Lodge, was built by Stephen Chesters-Thompson as part of the Horton Lodge development in 1890/91 and burnt down twice in the early 1890s. This is the 1895 version rebuilt by William Tellwright, owner of the Sneyd collieries. In the background is the boathouse built by the Challinor family from Leek in the late 1890s; a second storey was added by 1914.   *Author's collection*

Sandypoint boathouse, just south of the Lady of the Lake, was built c1914 by the Rigby family, who are seen here.

Rigby family collection

Views of railway trains taken from the Lake are very rare. Here is a Macclesfield to Uttoxeter working.in the mid-1950s.　　　　*Tim Shuttleworth*

The group of boathouses at the south end of the lake, a view taken in the 1920s. Only the three furthest boathouses still survive.   *Author's collection*

Four of the five boathouses can be seen in this 1905 view of the western shoreline in this Shaw of Burslem postcard.

Author's collection

George Heath's newly built landing stage c1908 to accommodate the growing number of visitors.

Author's collection

Extracted from 1906 NSR Tourist Guidebook.   *Author's collection*

C1900, thundering past the rocks at the south end of the lake is NSR 2-4-0 B Class locomotive No 22 at the head of an excursion train.   *Author's collection*

'Ivanhoe' seen here in front of the locomotive shed at Rudyard car park. The 10¼" narrow gauge line, opened in 1985 on the eastern side of the Lake, now runs for 1½ miles as far as Hunthouse Wood. This historic locomotive was built in 1937 by HCS Bullock, and incorporated parts of earlier locomotives dating back to the early 1900s. It arrived in Rudyard in 1987, was not heavily used and was then withdrawn from service in 1995.

Peter Hanton

Three of the leaflet guides to Rudyard Lake which have been produced over the years.

Author's collection

The Leek Ladies' Swimming Club taking to the cold water in this 1921 Harry Breaks' postcard.
Unwin family collection

Amateur Swimming Association 5 Kilometre Open Water Swimming Championships. which included trials for the 1997 European Championships at Seville. were held at Rudyard on 14 June 1997 as part of the Lake's bi-centennial celebrations.   *Author's collection*